Author's Dedication

To Master Evelyn Bell
of Oxford.

Evelyn Bell
I love you well.

Artist's Dedication

To Mrs. Ruth Brooks Heath
of Chestnut Hill.

I hereby bequeath
The pictures beneath
To Ruth Brooks Heath.

Child! do not throw this book about;
    Refrain from the unholy pleasure
Of cutting all the pictures out!
    Preserve it as your chiefest treasure.

Child, have you never heard it said
    That you are heir to all the ages?
Why, then, your hands were never made
    To tear these beautiful thick pages!

Your little hands were made to take
    The better things and leave the worse ones:
They also may be used to shake
    The Massive Paws of Elder Persons.

And when your prayers complete the day,
    Darling, your little tiny hands
Were also made, I think, to pray
    For men that lose their fairylands.

INTRODUCTION

I call you bad, my little child,
   Upon the title page,
Because a manner rude and wild
   Is common at your age.

The Moral of this priceless work
   (If rightly understood)
Will make you — from a little Turk —
   Unnaturally good.

Do not as evil children do,
  Who on the slightest grounds
Will imitate the Kangaroo,
  With wild unmeaning bounds.

Do not as children badly bred,
  Who eat like little Hogs,
And when they have to go to bed
  Will whine like Puppy Dogs:

Who take their manners from the Ape,
　　Their habits from the Bear,
Indulge the loud unseemly jape,
　　And never brush their hair.

But so control your actions that
Your friends may all repeat,
'This child is dainty as the Cat,
And as the owl discreet.'

The Yak
As a friend to the children commend me the Yak.

You will find it exactly the thing:
It will carry and fetch, you can ride on its back,
Or lead it about with a string.

The Tartar who dwells on the plains of Thibet
    (A desolate region of snow)
Has for centuries made it a nursery pet,
    And surely the Tartar should know!

Then tell your papa where the Yak can be got,
   And if he is awfully rich
He will buy you the creature — or else he will *not*.
   (I cannot be positive which.)

The Polar Bear

The Polar Bear is unaware
  Of cold that cuts me through:
For why? He has a coat of hair.
  I wish I had one too!

The Lion

The Lion, the Lion, he dwells in the waste,
He has a big head and a very small waist;
But his shoulders are stark, and his jaws they are grim,
And a good little child will not play with him.

The Tiger
The Tiger, on the other hand, is kittenish and mild,
He makes a pretty playfellow for any little child;

And mothers of large families (who claim to common sense)
Will find a Tiger well repay the trouble and expense.

The Dromedary

The Dromedary is a cheerful bird:
I cannot say the same about the Kurd.

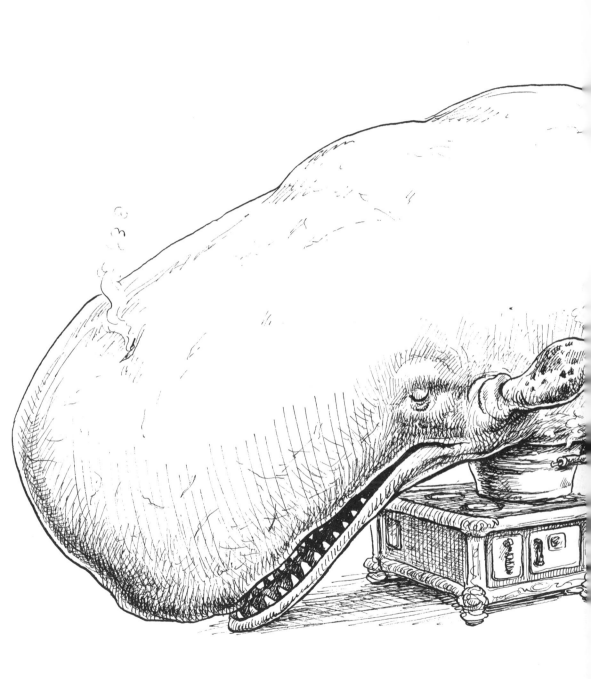

The Whale

The Whale that wanders round the Pole
  Is not a table fish.
You cannot bake or boil him whole,
  Nor serve him in a dish;

But you may cut his blubber up
And melt it down for oil,
And so replace the colza bean
(A product of the soil).

These facts should all be noted down
   And ruminated on,
By every boy in Oxford town
   Who wants to be a Don.

The Camel
"The Ship of the Desert."

THIS HIDE
CERTIFIED
PROOF AGAINST
STEEL, LEAD
PLATINUM,
TUNGSTEN AND
EGGPLANT

The Hippopotamus

I shoot the Hippopotamus with bullets made of platinum,
Because if I use leaden ones his hide is sure to flatten 'em.

The Dodo

The Dodo used to walk around,
  And take the sun and air.
The Sun yet warms his native ground —
  The Dodo is not there!

The voice which used to squawk and squeak
  Is now for ever dumb —
Yet may you see his bones and beak
  All in the Mu-se-um.

The Marmozet

The species Man and Marmozet
Are intimately linked;

The Marmozet survives as yet,
But Men are all extinct.

The Camelopard

The Camelopard, it is said
  By travellers (who never lie),
He cannot stretch out straight in bed
  Because he is so high.
The clouds surround his lofty head,
  His hornlets touch the sky.

How shall I hunt this quadruped?
  I cannot tell! Not I!
(A picture of how people try
  And fail to hit that head so high.)

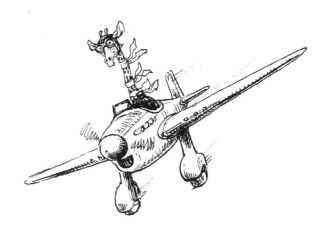

I'll buy a little parachute
  (A common parachute with wings),
I'll fill it full of arrowroot
  And other necessary things,
And I will slay this fearful brute
  With stones and sticks and guns and slings.
(A picture of how people shoot
  With comfort from a parachute.)

The Learned Fish

This Learned Fish has not sufficient brains
To go into the water when it rains.

The Elephant

When people call this beast to mind,
   They marvel more and more
At such a *LITTLE* tail behind,

So *LARGE* a trunk before.

The Big Baboon

The Big Baboon is found upon
   The plains of Cariboo;
He goes about with nothing on
   (A shocking thing to do.)
But if he dressed respectably
   And let his whiskers grow,

How like this Big Baboon would be
To Mister So-and-so!

The Rhinoceros

Rhinoceros, your hide looks all undone,
   You do not take my fancy in the least:
You have a horn where other brutes have none:
   Rhinoceros, you are an ugly beast.

The Frog

Be kind and tender to the Frog,
   And do not call him names,
As 'Slimy skin,' or 'Polly-wog',
   Or likewise 'Ugly James,'
Or 'Gape-a-grin,' or 'Toad-gone-wrong,'
   Or 'Billy Bandy-knees':
The Frog is justly sensitive
   To epithets like these.

No animal will more repay
   A treatment kind and fair;
At least so lonely people say
   Who keep a Frog (and, by the way,
They are extremely rare).

THE BAD CHILD'S
BOOK OF BEASTS

THE BAD CHILD'S
BOOK OF BEASTS

Verses by
Hilaire Belloc

Pictures by
Wallace Tripp

Sparhawk **Books Inc**
Pierce Crossing Road, Jaffrey, New Hampshire 03452

Belloc, Hilaire, 1870-1953.
  The Bad Child's Book of Beasts, was first published by
Duckworth and Company, London, in 1897.
  Summary: Humorous and cautionary verses about such
animals as the whale, the polar bear, the frog, the dodo, and
the yak.
  1. Animals — Juvenile poetry.   2. Children's poetry,
English.   3. Humorous poetry, English.
[1. Animals — Poetry. 2. Humorous poetry]
I. Tripp, Wallace, 1940-   ill.
II. Title.
PR6003.E45B3   1982   821'.912   82-5939
  ISBN 0-9605776-3-7 (pbk.)   AACR2

Illustrations copyright © 1982 by Wallace Tripp

  ISBN 0-9605776-3-7   First Edition 1982